HamsterDala
COLORING BOOK

Over 50
Hamster Mandalas
for inspiration,
mindfulness,
and fun

Laurren Darr

Left Paw Press

Contact us on our publisher's website at:
www.LeftPawPress.com

International Standard Book Number: 978-1-943356-34-8

PRINTED IN THE UNITED STATES OF AMERICA

Author: Laurren Darr

Cover design by Maria Charina Gomez.

Published and distributed by Left Paw Press, publishing imprint of
Lauren Originals, Inc. For educational, corporate, or retail sales accounts, email:
info@LeftPawPress.com.

For information, address: Left Paw Press 8926 N Greenwood Avenue #293 Niles, IL 60714.
Left Paw Press can be found on the web at
www.leftpawpress.com.

__Advantages of coloring__

Many promising studies have been conducted on art therapy. For those who are less inclined to create art as therapy and wanting a simpler solution, they are using coloring books to enrich their lives. Physicians and therapists prescribe coloring for many different illnesses including depression, PTSD, dementia, and even cancer patients to reduce their pain and stress levels in treatment.

Everyday, people are also looking for natural and joyful ways to lessen pain and reduce the tension in their lives. By coloring, the mind focuses. This, in turn, allows the brain to replace mind chatter and negative thoughts with positive thoughts. There are many benefits to having a coloring book routine, which include:

• Achieve a meditation state of mind. The alpha brain waves are present when the mind is sleeping or in a deep zen-like meditative state. When a person is coloring, the brain can get into this soothing, restorative mode.

• Assuage stress, worry, and fears. This happens in the amygdala portion of the brain where emotions and motivation are integrated. The amygdala gets calmed during the coloring process.

• Improve fine motor skills. This happens through the repetition of coloring and focusing on a task using your hands to stay within a finite area.

• Increase creativity. Coloring unlocks the right side of the brain and keeps it stimulated, allowing for more creative thoughts and solutions. This also leads to increased productivity.

• Relax, gain clarity, and focus. People can also reduce their blood pressure while coloring.

How to use this book

First of all, there is no wrong way of using this book to bring more peace to your life. There also is no right or wrong time or place to color. Taking the time to include creativity in your life will help with your well-being. This is the vision that I had when I set out to create *HamsterDala Coloring Book* and all the other Dala coloring books in the series. I wanted them to be of optimal benefit to anyone that got a copy. With that being said, onward!

Gather your materials. There is no particular medium to use. If you're drawn to colored pencils, crayons, markers, or paint, go with the flow. You may also decide to use different materials at different times. I have a long desk in my office that has a mixture of all of these. I grab whatever 'strikes my fancy.'

Thumb through the HamsterDalas and pick one that piques your interest. Some people like to keep the book together and others like to cut the page out to color it. Again, it's whatever works best for you. It's also appropriate to note that it doesn't matter whether you complete the HamsterDala or not. Color until you feel 'complete.'

You'll also find that, the pages opposite the HamsterDalas have a mantra. These affirmations are included as a suggestion to meditate on while coloring. You'll find that they are repeated in the background to represent how people mentally repeat a mantra over and over. These are also faded so that you can include your own colored notes on what that HamsterDala and mantra brought up for you. However, if this is something that doesn't resonate with you, no worries. I can't stress enough to follow your energy and color in a way that feels best and is most appealing to you.

Most importantly, have fun coloring, relaxing, and taking time to include creativity in your life! Allow *HamsterDala Coloring Book* to bring you joy!

Lauren

I am at peace...I am at peace...I am at peace...I am at peace...I
am at peace...I am at peace...I am at peace...I am at peace...I
am at peace...I am at peace...I am at peace...I am at peace...I
am at peace...I am at peace...I am at peace...I am at peace...I
am at peace...I am at peace...I am at peace...I am at peace...I
am at peace...I am at peace...I am at peace...I am at peace...I
am at peace...I am at peace...I am at peace...I am at peace...I

I am at peace...

am at peace...I am at peace...I am at peace...I am at peace...I
am at peace...I am at peace...I am at peace...I am at peace...I
am at peace...I am at peace...I am at peace...I am at peace...I
am at peace...I am at peace...I am at peace...I am at peace...I
am at peace...I am at peace...I am at peace...I am at peace...I
am at peace...I am at peace...I am at peace...I am at peace...I
am at peace...I am at peace... I am at peace...I am at peace...I
am at peace...I am at peace...I am at peace...I am at peace...I
am at peace...I am at peace...I am at peace...I am at peace...I
am at peace... I am at peace...I am at peace...I am at peace...I
am at peace... I am at peace...I am at peace...I am at peace...I
am at peace... I am at peace...I am at peace...I am at peace...I

I love and accept myself completely... I love and accept myself completely... I love and accept myself completely... I love and accept myself completely... I love and accept myself completely... I love and accept myself completely... I love and accept myself completely... I love and accept myself completely... I love and accept myself completely... I love and accept myself completely... I love and accept myself completely...

I love and accept myself completely...

I love and accept myself completely... I love and accept myself

I allow myself to dream...

I am surrounded by love...

I am healthy, wealthy, and wise...

I choose happiness...

I love my life... I love my life... I love my life... I love my life... I love my
life... I love my life... I love my life... I love my life... I love my life... I love
my life... I love my life... I love my life... I love my life... I love my life... I love
life... I love my life... I love my life... I love my life... I love my life... I love my
I love my life... I love my life... I love my life... I love my life... I love my life...
my life... I love my life... I love my life... I love my life... I love my life... I lov
life... I love my life... I love my life... I love my life... I love my life... I love my
I love my life... I love my life... I love my life... I love my life... I love my life...
my life... I love my life... I love my life... I love my life... I love my life... I lov
life... I love my life... I love my life... I love my life... I love my life... I love my
I love my life... I love my life... I love my life... I love my life... I love my life...
my life... I love my life... I love my life... I love my life... I love my life... I lov
life... I love my life... I love my life... I love my life... I love my life... I love my
I love my life... I love my life... I love my life... I love my life... I love my life...
my life... I love my life... I love my life... I love my life... I love my life... I lov
life... I love my life... I love my life... I love my life... I love my life... I love my
I love my life... I love my life... I love my life... I love my life... I love my life...
my life... I love my life... I love my life... I love my life... I love my life... I lov
I love my life... I love my life... I love my life... I love my life... I love my life...

I am open...

I deserve all that is good in the world...

...serve all that is good in the world... I deserve all that is good
e world... I deserve all that is good in the world... I deserve all
is good in the world... I deserve all that is good in the world...
serve all that is good in the world... I deserve all that is good
e world... I deserve all that is good in the world... I deserve all
is good in the world... I deserve all that is good in the world...
serve all that is good in the world... I deserve all that is good
e world... I deserve all that is good in the world... I deserve all
is good in the world... I deserve all that is good in the world...
serve all that is good in the world... I deserve all that is good
e world... I deserve all that is good in the world... I deserve all
is good in the world... I deserve all that is good in the world...
serve all that is good in the world... I deserve all that is good
e world... I deserve all that is good in the world... I deserve all
is good in the world... I deserve all that is good in the world...
serve all that is good in the world... I deserve all that is good
e world... I deserve all that is good in the world... I deserve all
is good in the world... I deserve all that is good in the world...
serve all that is good in the world... I deserve all that is good in
world... I deserve all that is good in the world... I deserve all

I am in
the flow...

I bring love and joy to everything I do...

I am
confident

I am free to make my own choices and decisions...

I am calm...

I am
successful...

I am healthy and balanced... I am healthy and balanced... I am
healthy and balanced... I am healthy and balanced... I am healthy
and balanced... I am healthy and balanced... I am healthy and
balanced... I am healthy and balanced... I am healthy and
balanced... I am healthy and balanced... I am healthy and
balanced... I am healthy and balanced... I am healthy and
balanced... I am healthy and balanced... I am healthy and
balanced... I am healthy and balanced... I am healthy and
balanced... I am healthy and balanced... I am healthy and
balanced... I am healthy and balanced... I am healthy and
balanced... I am healthy and balanced... I am healthy and
balanced... I am healthy and balanced... I am healthy and
balanced... I am healthy and balanced... I am healthy and
balanced... I am healthy and balanced... I am healthy and
balanced... I am healthy and balanced... I am healthy and
balanced... I am healthy and balanced... I am healthy and
balanced... I am healthy and balanced... I am healthy and
balanced... I am healthy and balanced... I am healthy and
balanced... I am healthy and balanced... I am healthy and
balanced... I am healthy and balanced... I am healthy and

I am healthy and balanced....

I honor myself at all times...

I have been blessed in this body...

I learn from all of my experiences...

I am grateful for everything in my life...

I value myself...

I am a magnet for miracles...

I release all worries... I release all worries... I release all worries...
I release all worries... I release all worries... I release all worries...
I release all worries... I release all worries... I release all worries...

I release all worries...

I release all worries... I release all worries... I release all worries...
I release all worries... I release all worries... I release all worries...
I release all worries... I release all worries... I release all worries...
I release all worries... I release all worries... I release all worries...
I release all worries... I release all worries... I release all worries...
I release all worries... I release all worries... I release all worries...
I release all worries... I release all worries... I release all worries...
I release all worries... I release all worries... I release all worries...
I release all worries... I release all worries... I release all worries...
I release all worries... I release all worries... I release all worries...
I release all worries... I release all worries... I release all worries...
I release all worries... I release all worries... I release all worries...
I release all worries... I release all worries... I release all worries...
I release all worries... I release all worries... I release all worries...
I release all worries... I release all worries... I release all worries...

I am proud of myself...

I am worthy...

I choose prosperity...

I am more than enough... just as I am...

I am safe and secure...

I appreciate all of my experiences...

I trust my higher self...

I am financially secure...

I am alive and filled with vitality...

I radiate love and joy to everyone I meet...

I nourish myself...

I have an open
mind...

I deserve a happy and prosperous life...

I believe in unlimited possibilities...

I am the creator of my success...

I am all that I can be...

I feel oneness with all of life...

I love today...
It is a great
day...

I am a blessing... I am a blessing... I am a blessing... I am a blessing...
I am a blessing... I am a blessing... I am a blessing... I am a blessing...
I am a blessing... I am a blessing... I am a blessing... I am a blessing...

I am a blessing...

I am a blessing... I am a blessing... I am a blessing... I am a blessing...
I am a blessing... I am a blessing... I am a blessing... I am a blessing...
I am a blessing... I am a blessing... I am a blessing... I am a blessing...
I am a blessing... I am a blessing... I am a blessing... I am a blessing...
I am a blessing... I am a blessing... I am a blessing... I am a blessing...
I am a blessing... I am a blessing... I am a blessing... I am a blessing...
I am a blessing... I am a blessing... I am a blessing... I am a blessing...
I am a blessing... I am a blessing... I am a blessing... I am a blessing...
I am a blessing... I am a blessing... I am a blessing... I am a blessing...
I am a blessing... I am a blessing... I am a blessing... I am a blessing...
I am a blessing... I am a blessing... I am a blessing... I am a blessing...
I am a blessing... I am a blessing... I am a blessing... I am a blessing...
I am a blessing... I am a blessing... I am a blessing... I am a blessing...

I am filled
with pure
positive energy...

I am motivated to reach my goals...

I deserve to be financially free and independent...

I am worthy of prosperity, joy, and love...

I attract all things that I desire in my life....

I possess the wisdom and power to accomplish anything...

I hold the keys to my destiny...

I have fun all the time...

I am beautiful...

beautiful... I am beautiful...I am beautiful... I am beautiful...
beautiful...I am beautiful...I am beautiful... I am beautiful...
beautiful... I am beautiful...I am beautiful... I am beautiful...
beautiful...I am beautiful...I am beautiful... I am beautiful...
beautiful... I am beautiful...I am beautiful... I am beautiful...
beautiful...I am beautiful...I am beautiful... I am beautiful...
beautiful... I am beautiful...I am beautiful... I am beautiful...
beautiful...I am beautiful...I am beautiful... I am beautiful...
beautiful... I am beautiful...I am beautiful... I am beautiful...
beautiful...I am beautiful...I am beautiful... I am beautiful...
beautiful... I am beautiful...I am beautiful... I am beautiful...
beautiful...I am beautiful...I am beautiful... I am beautiful...
beautiful... I am beautiful...I am beautiful... I am beautiful...
beautiful...I am beautiful...I am beautiful... I am beautiful...
beautiful... I am beautiful...I am beautiful... I am beautiful...
beautiful...I am beautiful...I am beautiful... I am beautiful...

Get the most comprehensive dog fashion illustrations set along with design considerations in the Dog Breeds Pet Fashion Illustration Encyclopedia book set. Includes all of the AKC breeds separated by the seven breed groups.

Coming 2017!

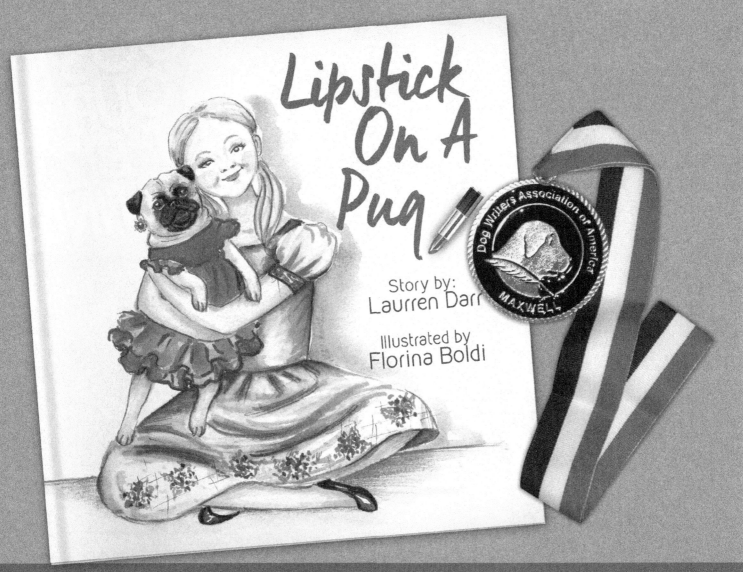

Learn about the roots of Laurren's plumb pug craziness and obsession with pet fashion in this children's book that will teach about the love of dog, pet rescue, and the unbreakable bonds between humans and their pets.

Lipstick On A Pug won the 2015 Children's Book of the Year Maxwell Medallion from the Dog Writers Association of America.

Also available in coloring book format

TAMBIÉN EN ESPAÑOL

BOOST YOUR PET BIZ MARKETING!

Unleashable
TURBO BOOST

Get the ultimate trade show conference 'in a box' with timeless interviews conducted for the Unleashable summit. You'll gain amazing marketing and industry insights from several different high profile people in the pet industry. Interviews include the following:

Pet Industry Attorney
Pet Industry Publisher
Pet Industry PR Person & FIT Professor
Pet Industry Trade Show Executive
Pet Industry Editor-in-Chief
Pet Industry Video Producer
Pet Model Stylist
Pet Blogger
Pet Industry Financial Executive

Find out more information at **www.PetFashionProfessionals.com**

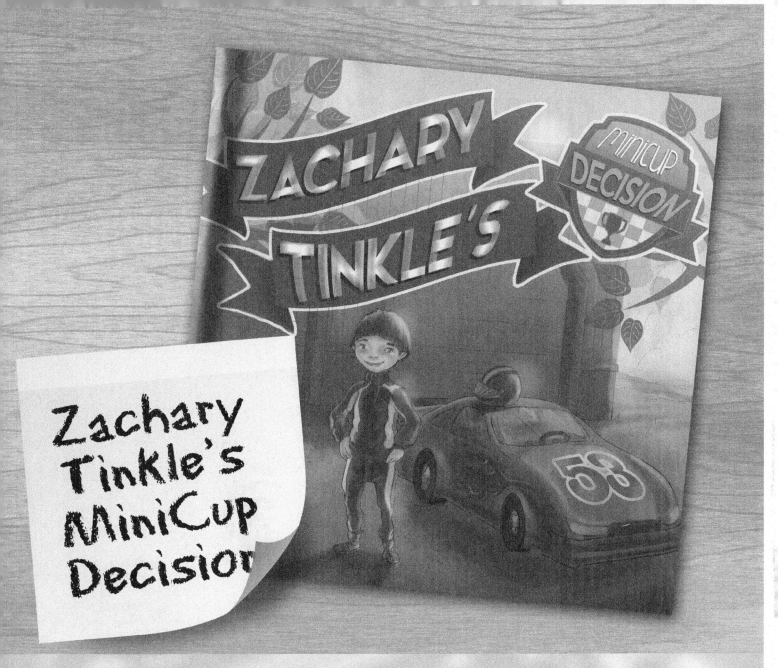

Zachary Tinkle wants to be a NASCAR® driver when he grows up, so he's been practicing with go-karts, getting ready for his first time racing outdoors. But when his parents take him to get the autograph of a famous NASCAR® driver, he sees something he can't believe: A little NASCAR® stock car-just his size. It's a minicup, a half-size stock car that can go 100 miles per hour on the track. Then he meets a father and his young son-who races a mincup! Zachary loves go-karts, but he knows a mincup will get him to the NASCAR big leagues. It's time to make a decision, and talk to Mom and Dad... Children and race fans will love this account by Zachary Tinkle, based on his own true-life story. It's about working hard for your dreams, and the value of thinking through important decisions.

TAMBIÉN
EN
ESPAÑOL

www.LeftPawPress.com

PUG CHILDREN'S FAIRY TALE SERIES
BOOKS ARE AVAILABLE IN
COLOR AND COLORING BOOK VERSIONS

Zachary Tinkle

2015 Short Track Auto Racing Series
Illinois State MiniCup Champion

Rainbow Rocket paint scheme

53

**Left Paw Press
is a
Proud Sponsor
Zachary Tinkle**
MiniCup Stock Car Driver

    DIYMARKETING.tv

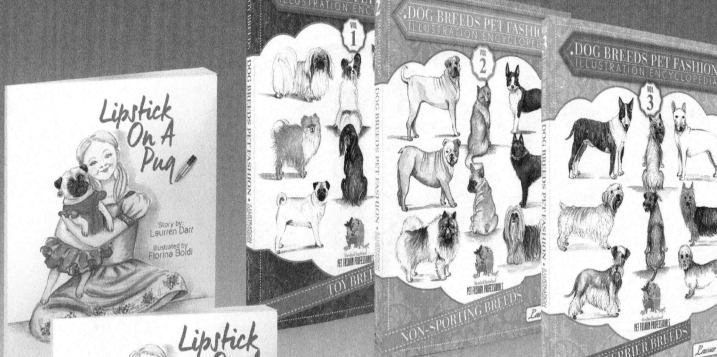

About The Author

Laurren Darr has been a plumb-pug-crazy, animal-loving, pet fashionologist and creative since childhood. She immerses herself in expression through writing and art. She's found that including visionary habits in life is beneficial to health while feeding the soul. Darr is on a mission to unleash the human animal bond and connection through imaginative processes highlighting pets and empowering pet fashion professionals.

She has over twenty years of marketing experience and has been an entrepreneur since 2004, creating the publishing imprint Left Paw Press in 2008. She has consulted with companies of all sizes specializing in trade show marketing. Laurren has won over 40 marketing awards and is a #1 best-selling author. Her book, <u>Lipstick On A Pug</u>, won the Maxwell Medallion from the Dog Writers Association of America in 2015 for Children's Book of the Year.

In August 2013, Laurren combined her marketing experience and lifelong love of pet fashionology to launch International Association of Pet Fashion Professionals, an organization created to provide tools to the pet fashion industry. She's been named a "Paw-er Woman" by the Fidose of Reality blog and was a 2015 & 16 finalist for Pet Industry Woman of the Year by Women In The Pet Industry.

Laurren also completed her pet fashion certification from FIT.

Laurren's busy home is filled with her geneticist husband, her son, Zachary Tinkle, who is a rising stock car racing star, and her fabulously fashionable fawn pug, Bella.

CPSIA information can be obtained
at www.ICGtesting.com
Printed in the USA
BVOW04s1658201117
500675BV00038B/347/P